MY GREAT BRITISH PIER TRIP

66 Seaside Piers in 21 days

Chris Foote Wood

*Chris sports his
"end of the pier" costume*

Chris's amusing day-by-day report in words and pictures of his travels around the
UK coast visiting all our surviving seaside piers.

ISBN 978-0-9553869-4-7

Published 2008 by Northern Writers, Bishop Auckland
Second Edition 2009

Front cover: Hastings Pier; Back Cover: Saltburn Pier

First published in 2008 by Northern Writers "Wor Hoos" 28 Cockton Hill Road
Bishop Auckland County Durham DL14 6AH
www.writersinc.biz

British Library Cataloguing in Publication Data
A catalogue for this book is available from the British Library.

ISBN 978-0-9553869-4-7

Produced & Edited by Chris Foote Wood at footewood@btconnect.com

Typeset in 10/12pt Garamond
Typesetting and origination, printed and bound by Lintons Printers Ltd, Beechburn, Crook, Co Durham DL15 8RA
www.lintons-printers.co.uk

Ramsey Queens 2007, pier in the morning sun

My Great British Pier Trip

INTRODUCTION

This book is a record - in words and pictures - of my 2007 "Pier Trip" around all the remaining seaside piers in England, Wales and the Isle of Man. I counted 56 "proper" piers, that is, those with extra facilities other than just "walking over the waves". My pier odyssey was something I had been wanting to do for fifty years or more. So why did I wait that long? To find out, read on.

"Blogs" are all the rage now - I've even tried them myself - so this account is in effect a Piers Blog. It took me 21 days to visit 66 piers in all - 67 if you count Wigan Pier, which I do mention, you'll be pleased to note. I must confess this was not a continuous (and strenuous) three weeks. This Pier trip was spread over several months - my more relaxed lifestyle after disposing of my 24/7, 364 days a year North Press Agency not yet allowing me the luxury of three weeks off.

As well as this book, there are two other things I want to tell you about. One is my "proper" Piers Book, a complete compendium of all the 56 seaside pleasure piers I visited on my 2007 round-Britain trip. It's called "Walking over the Waves - Quintessential British Seaside Piers". In addition to details of all 56 piers, it includes the history of each pier, the people who built and ran them, the showbiz stars who performed on them, and many tales of storms, fires and shipwrecks, together with 300+ old and new photographs and postcards. The other thing I want you to take note of is the Great British Pier Crawl 2008. This is a fun competition, free to enter. Visit a minimum of three seaside piers in the UK and you qualify as a Midshipman PierCrawler. More than three, and you can work your way up to Captain or even Admiral. Certificates of your PierCrawler Rank cost £2 including postage. *[2009 Note: you can still do the PierCrawl at any time!]* Thank you for reading my blog book

Chris Foote Wood

To get my book "Walking Over the Waves" (ISBN 9781904445678) go to any good bookshop, or buy on line via www.writersinc.biz

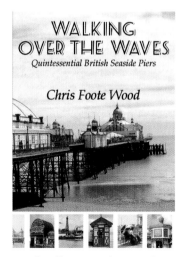

"Walking over the Waves"

CONTENTS

PIERS INDEX

Chapter One

Toe in the water

SALTBURN (1869)

A cold morning in Saltburn - this is where I start my odyssey around the coast of Britain. Well, the North Sea's always cold, isn't it? Something about the North East coast facing the Russian steppes, and the Gulf Stream being on the other side of the country. When you set out to visit all our surviving seaside piers, you have to start somewhere, so why not the one nearest home? My nearest pier is at Saltburn, or rather Saltburn-by-the-Sea. These seaside resorts do insist on adding "by the Sea" or "on Sea" after their names, sometimes with hyphens and sometimes not, according to taste. And they can get shirty if you miss off the "Sea" bit.

If you must know, I live in Bishop Auckland in County Durham. Before the powers-that-be started to fiddle with our ancient county boundaries, Durham included everything between the River Tyne and the River Tees, and that's the way I still think of it – and so do a lot of other people too. "Bishop" lies in the exact geographical centre of County Durham, so it's a little way off the sea. As far as I'm concerned, Saltburn is in North Yorkshire, and boasts Yorkshire's only remaining pier – and a fine pier it is too.

Saltburn 2007, from cliff top

I arrive in Saltburn early on a bright Spring morning. After stopping off at the station – yes, Saltburn still has its railway as well as its pier – for some much-needed refreshment and the essential toilet break, I venture along to the cliff top to be rewarded with a terrific view of this newly-restored pier from above. Most piers you have to view from the flat, and as good as that is, you can't beat looking down from above. Apart from taking some sort of aerial transport, a hang-glider or hot-air balloon, there are not many piers you can look right down on. Mumbles is another one that comes to mind, but that involves taking your life in your hands as you scramble up Mumbles Head, mountain-goat fashion.

Saltburn Pier has a distinctive red-and-white livery. It is beautifully kept, and there are no "amusements" on the pier deck – much shortened since its heyday. But the best part is the cliff lift, the oldest water-powered lift in the UK, if not the world, as the three likely lads who were busy preparing for the 10am opening time were only too pleased to tell me. Alan, Dave and Norman are incredibly cheerful and clearly enjoy their work. They let me take a sneaky look inside the bowels of the lift machinery. The lift is controlled by

Saltburn 2007, top station, cliff lift

a disc brake. There's never been an accident, I was relieved to hear. As proof, the old disc brake wheel is on display at the top of the bank. It did service for 114 years without a hitch, before being replaced in 1998. The Victorians certainly built things to last!

The way the lift operates is simple. There are two tracks and two cars, connected by a loop. To fetch people up from the bottom, water is pumped into a tank underneath the top car until it is just heavy enough to go down under gravity and braking, thus bringing up the bottom car. The cars themselves are a joy to behold, and the top cabin, with its interesting controls, is a little gem. My walk time: 2min 11sec. Later I get to meet Tony Lynn of the Friends of Saltburn Pier. He is a mine of information, and not just about Saltburn and its pier. We enjoy a coffee at one of several places along the sea front that are now opening to take advantage of the increasing numbers of visitors to this quiet and pleasant resort with its cliff views.

Saltburn 2007, lift cars

Chapter Two

Down the East Coast

CLEETHORPES (1873)

It was the middle of June when I set out on a three-day trip to "recce" all the piers on the East Coast, from Cleethorpes to Southend. This was the real start of my odyssey, and if you're going to visit seaside piers you can't do better than to get advice from a man who knows – in my case, Tim Mickleburgh. Now I'm not saying this just because Tim has helped me with my book "Walking over the Waves", but he has a terrific pedigree. Tim has been involved in the National Piers Society for many years. He has written several books on piers, including the "Guide to British Piers" which has been my guide throughout. Tim lives in Scunthorpe, and Cleethorpes is his closest pier, so it makes sense for us to meet there. Not that there was any chance of us missing each other. Cleethorpes is one of no fewer than four UK piers, each claiming to be the shortest. It certainly is very short, so after viewing the pier we adjourn to the local library for our editorial conference.

The pavilion on Cleethorpes Pier (there's only room for one!) is called "Pier 39" after a famous pier at San Francisco. I thought the whole pier was called Pier 39, but pier manager Robbie Marklew tells me this is not so. He is developing the Pavilion as an

Cleethorpes 2007

Cromer 2007

entertainment centre and has various groups playing there. The pier may be short, but the promenade is long with lots of shops and amusements, and there's plenty of parking. To get about, there's the road train which charges £1 a time ("all classes, one way"). Tim tells me about the Humberstone "Fitties" which were small houses used mainly as second homes not far from the sea. My walk time: 60secs.

SKEGNESS (1881)

Next pier down the coast is at Skegness, which always brings to mind the famous poster with its skipping sailor and the line "Skegness – it's so bracing". One thing I forgot to mention about the East Coast: nearly all our seaside resorts have lots and lots of

Skegness 2007, roomy deck

lovely sandy beaches. Same with the West Coast. And Wales. And quite a few in the South West. But on the South Coast, pebbles are generally the order of the day. But my task was to clock all our piers, East, South and West, so I just mention this in passing. Getting from Cleethorpes to Skegness, I take the inland route along the A16 via Louth. This means I by-pass Mablethorpe, which is a pity as I've never been there. It's a funny thing, but I always think it's easier to travel from North to South. I know it's daft, but I have this idea that going N-S is somehow going downhill, freewheeling as it were. But I must get to Great Yarmouth by nightfall, so I have to crack on. A few photographs, a few notes, and quick walk along the pier, and I am once more on my way. My walk time: 1min 13sec.

CROMER (1901)

From "Skeggy", I take the A52 to Boston where I am held up a little in the rush-hour traffic. Then it's the A17, skirting the Wash to King's Lynn. No need to go to Hunstanton on the east side of the wash, as it no longer has its pier. It's straight on via the A148 to Cromer which is on the north-east corner of Norfolk. It was just starting to get dark by the time I arrived in Cromer. This is another pier you can view from above, and a very handsome pier it is too, and it has a theatre. Overlooking the pier are several hotels, including the very posh-sounding Hotel de Paris. The entrance to the pier has a sinuous set of steps commemorating the heroic deeds of the Cromer lifeboatmen. The slipway and boathouse are being upgraded to accommodate a new £2.5m Tamar class lifeboat "currently in build" at Plymouth. Meantime, a Mersey class lifeboat was doing duty. A recent rescue is recorded thus: *"On Thursday May 10th 2007, the lifeboat Royal Shipwright was launched at 09:50hrs to go to the rescue of the ex-fishing vessel Annelise. With two people on board, it had engine problems and was taking on water. The vessel was escorted until the engines eventually failed and the lifeboat then towed the vessel to Great Yarmouth around 16:00 hrs"*. It bears repeating that the RNLI is funded entirely by donations from the public.

Resisting the urge to have a drink on the pier – I still had a way to drive – I complete my walk in the gathering gloom. There's something quite romantic about the sight and sound of white-tipped waves breaking on the beach in the dark, but my dear wife Frances is not with me and I have to move on. Whenever I travel without her, Frances is always with me in spirit. She reinforces this with a telephone call every

Great Yarmouth Britannia 2007

Great Yarmouth Britannia c1930

Great Yarmouth Jetty 1926

Great Yarmouth Jetty 2007

*Great Yarmouth Wellington 2008,
brand new pavilion*

*Great Yarmouth Wellington 2007,
Winter Gardens on left*

evening to check on my progress and to tell me what a tough day she's had at the office while I've been gadding about enjoying myself. "But it's not the same without you, love," I always say, but somehow I don't think she believes me. My walk time: 1min 48sec.

GREAT YARMOUTH BRITANNIA (1858)

Not wanting to get stuck in the environs of Norwich, I take the A149 through North Walsam. It's pitch black when I get to Great Yarmouth. Of course you can enjoy a pier at night, the bright lights and all the fun of the fair. But I had a serious task, to have a good look at every pier and to "walk the planks" from end to end. In any case, I was pretty whacked after all my endeavours and was glad to bed down at my pre-arranged hotel. Isn't the internet wonderful? Nowadays I book everything on the net, and why they didn't think of it fifty years ago I can't imagine. It must be good for the businesses involved, getting orders from the ether. Now I'm not going to "diss" any of the places I've stayed at, so don't expect any horror stories. As you can imagine, some have been better than others, but the inexpensive ones (I won't say cheap) have all provided basic accommodation for a modest fee, and the occasional more upmarket establishment has done the business. What I hadn't taken into account was the fact that breakfast at my Great Yarmouth "gaff" didn't start until 9am, and I was wanting to be "up and doing" long before then.

So off I go with no brekky for an early reconnaissance of Great Yarmouth's two piers. If you didn't know it before, that's where the word recce comes from. But I am stymied in my pier studies. Of course, I should have realized that most piers don't open until 9am at the earliest. So I could have stayed in bed and had a late breakfast, but the die is cast. I sneak onto to Britannia Pier in the guess of a workman or some such, and almost made it to the end of the pier when I was spotted, sussed and ordered off. But I'd seen what I wanted to see, although my walk time was inevitably a little less than it should have been. My walk time: 2min 21sec.

GREAT YARMOUTH JETTY

Then it's along the promenade to take a look at Great Yarmouth's other pier, the Wellington. But what's this? Midway between the two piers is the Great Yarmouth Jetty. A modest structure, certainly, but it does stretch out into the sea, and it has seats, a telescope and even a lamppost. But does it qualify as a pier? Lacking any form of amusements and with it being so small, sadly the Jetty does not qualify. But I walk it just the same. My walk time: 1min 29sec.

GREAT YARMOUTH WELLINGTON (1853)

Great Yarmouth Wellington Pier is the older of the town's two pleasure piers. It was also closed, but for the very good reason that it's being rebuilt. As usual, the pavilion is flourishing and offers plenty of amusements. The huge timbers standing proud out of the sand are something to behold, but sadly I had no pier to walk along. So no walk time, then. *[2009 Note: the Pavilion has since been rebuilt, looking exactly like the original]*.

LOWESTOFT CLAREMONT (1903)

Then on to Lowestoft just down the coast where, joy oh joy, there are also two piers. I tootle past the South Pier to first have a look at the Claremont Pier which is close by. The pier itself is closed, but the shore facilities are fully functional, and just as well. Captain Nemo's Restaurant provides an excellent vegetarian breakfast and much-needed toilet facilities. Wasn't Captain Nemo that bloke who? Yes, he was the captain of the Nautilus in Jules Verne's ripping yarn "20,000 Leagues under the Sea". He was an adventurer, a bit of a mystery man. And he kept a good table – the food, not the furniture. But, sadly, this pier is in a bad way and needs a lorra lorra cash spending on it. Here's hoping. So no walk time, again.

Lowestoft South 2008, lively front

Lowestoft Claremont 2007, deck closed

Lowestoft South, East Point Pavilion

LOWESTOFT SOUTH (1846)

But Lowestoft South Pier makes up for it with an interesting walk along the harbour groin, because that's what South Pier is in fact. But South Pier looks like a pier, sounds like a pier, and has all the pier facilities, so it must be a pier - despite having no legs. My walk time: 3min 24sec.

SOUTHWOLD (1900)

There is just enough daylight left for me to have a good look at Southwold Pier, a few miles down the coast. Any pier that advertises "The Under the Pier Show" has got to be good, and it is. There are so many strange and peculiar things on this pier, you really do need to go and look for yourselves. I particularly like

Southwold 2007, Quantum Tunnelling Telescope

"The Quantum Tunnelling Telescope". The Rev Charles Dodgson (Lewis Carroll – author of Alice in Wonderland etc) would have been at home on Southwold. Or maybe he did visit....? *[2009 Note: after all, Southwold was good enough for prime minister Gordon Brown to have his hols here].* There's nothing peculiar about the Boardwalk Café, it's just really nice and as always it's a great pleasure to eat and drink "Over the Waves". Southwold itself looks very well. There's a gem of a boating lake close by the pier with yet another inviting tea-room. My only beef is that the toilets in the council car-park are closed – but there are "Facilities" on the pier. My walk time: 2min 08sec.

Now this is where my itinerary goes all wrong, or I have a "cunning plan" – take your pick. My resting-place for the night is the Waverley Hotel in Felixstowe. Next day I am up early, as usual. It's funny how I just cannot lie in bed of a morning even if I don't have to get up. It's sort of sinful, and doubly so because it's so enjoyable lying in your nice warm bed. So I do get up early, have an excellent breakfast at the Waverley, and set off early, to Clacton. I ignore Felixstowe Pier for the time being, knowing it is closed at this early hour and that it will still be there when I got back. Now you may say I'm adding to the mileage, but time is money and as I'm self-employed, it's my time I'm looking to save. I can stay away from my home/office HQ in Bishop Auckland only so long. Besides, I like to crack on and can't abide hanging around, filling in time. So Clacton it is.

14

Clacton 2007, pier approach

Clacton c1910

Walton-on-the-Naze, bold front

Walton-on-the-Naze 2007, the bend at the end of Britain's second-longest seaside pier

CLACTON (1871)

Clacton Pier is well under way when I get there. This is a real seaside pleasure pier, catering for the masses (that includes me!). The "Cockney Pride" pub gives you a clue as to where the masses mainly used to come from, good old London Town. To its great credit, Tendring District Council is promoting walking for health and pleasure. Pedant CFW can't help noticing the dreaded apostrophe in café's but who cares when you're having a good time? My walk time: 3min 28sec.

WALTON-ON-THE-NAZE (1871)

Warning: Walton Pier, the pier with the bend at the end, is very, very long. It's the third longest pier in the country, after Southend and Southport. But it's worth the walk, if only to see the RNLI Tyne Class lifeboat Sir Galahad snugly moored in its new station at the end of the pier. Being parked there, a long way from the shore, means that emergency response times are shorter. So it's not just anglers and pigeons who camp out on the end of the pier. Why do the pigeons camp out there? It's a mystery to me. The lifeboat is protected by a new wave screen. Built in 2005, it consists of slats that let the waves through while reducing much of their power – really effective. This is the same principle that the great engineer Isambard Kingdom Brunel used to protect his huge ship, the SS Great Britain, when it was stranded on Dundrum Bay beach near Belfast in 1846 and was stuck for several months before it could be floated off on an exceptionally high tide. Without the screen to protect it, this huge ship would have been pounded to pieces by the waves. My walk time: 7min 49sec.

FELIXSTOWE (1905)

Retracing my steps to Felixstowe, I enter the pier via the amusement arcade only to find I can go no further. "Danger – no access beyond this point", despite the fact that it looks in good condition. But ours is not to reason why. There's the arcade and the leisure centre nearby, plus shops and cafes across the road, so plenty for visitors. But pier enthusiasts like me are denied the pleasure of walking over the waves. My walk time (arcade only): 34sec.

Felixstowe 2007

Southend 2007, vanishing point

*Southend 2008, Sir William Heygate pier train
(the other is John Betjeman)*

Southend Jetty 2007, Ness Road slipway

Southend Corporation Loading Pier 2007, since demolished

SOUTHEND-ON-SEA (1830/1890)

Now for the big one, the biggest of them all. To get to Southend it's a long drive past Ipswich, Colchester and Chelmsford, but perhaps that's appropriate. Southend Pier is the longest in the UK and the longest in the world – one and a third miles long. Just as well there's a railway! Actually, having a railway along it doubles the interest in a pier, at least for me. So I take the train to the end of the pier and walk back. Southend Pier has had more than its fair share of fires, and some of them have been spectacular as well as hugely damaging. You can see quite a number of charred timbers, and on my visit I find the pier-end railway terminus is a temporary one due to the recent fire. But Southend pier has always come back, better than ever.

I contact the lady in charge of the pier, Southend Borough Council resort manager Lynn Jones and we arrange to meet, on the pier of course. She is charming (I'm not just saying that!) and very helpful. Later I contact another very important lady in the life of Southend Pier, Peggy Dowie. Peggy is chairman of the Friends of Southport Pier, and she too is very helpful. The new viewing platform which links the town with the pier – it includes lifts to all floors – is the best place to view the pier. But Southend Pier is so long, it's almost impossible to get a good photograph of the whole structure as it sticks out (so it would seem) half way across the Thames Estuary. But I have seen it from the air, and that is a spectacular view. My walk time: 20min 14sec.

Just downstream there are two "piers" that are not really piers. One is a derelict wharf, 150-200 metres long and 15 metres wide. So it is a pier, but not a pleasure pier. *[2009 Note: it has since been demolished]*. And the other one is the Ness Road Slipway where permitted launching is allowed for "personalized water craft". But along the Esplanade, there are severe warnings that "no water-skiing, aqua-planing, para-kiting or similar activities within 200 metres of a wharf, jetty, public beach, bathing place or residential property". That just about covers everything, I think. But there's more. *"Mechanically-propelled craft, including wet bikes, may not be launched from the sea-wall and in the Ray Gut at low water. Maximum fine £200"*.

Here endeth my "promenade" along the eastern seaboard, taking in twelve "proper" piers and a few more land-sea structures. It's been fun, but quite tough. Now for the North West coast.

Chapter Three

West Coast Blues

Knott End

Now I don't want to complain. For all that I was born in Cheshire and brought up in Lancashire, I've got to admit – it does rain in the North West. A lot - it's just nature. Apparently, the storm clouds roll over the Atlantic, picking up moisture, before depositing it on the North West. Maybe that's why I've settled in the North East – it's dryer. But the rain never stopped me having a great time as a youngster, with many, many trips to the coast – Liverpool, Southport, Lytham, Blackpool, Fleetwood, Knott End, Morecambe. Never heard of Knott End? You should go there. Take the ferry from Fleetwood. So you can guess that when I revisited my old holiday haunts on the North West coast, it rained. Well, some of the time. There's no longer a pier at New Brighton – that's across the Mersey from Liverpool – so I kick off my North West tour at Southport. But first just I had to stop off at the pier that's the most famous in the world for not being a pier atall – Wigan Pier.

WIGAN PIER

Living in Bury, not too many miles from Wigan, I first heard about Wigan Pier at Alderman Smith's Infants School. "There really is a pier at Wigan," said an older lad, and I believed him.

Knott End 2007, ferry about to return to Fleetwood

Wigan 2007, what's left of the pier

19

And it's true! There is a pier at Wigan, but not as we know it, Jim. If you want to see Wigan Pier, you can. It's well-signposted, off the M6. Wigan Pier was jokingly made famous around 1900 by Lancashire comedian George Formby senior. More recently, George Orwell (Eric Blair) who wrote "Animal Farm" and "1984" also wrote "The Road to Wigan Pier". The Pier – or what's left of it – can still be seen. It's a raised platform at the side of the Liverpool-Leeds canal. It was in fact a "coal shute" or coaling station where barges used to load up with coal from the local pits for onward transmission to Liverpool and export to Ireland and America. There were a number of such "piers" on the canal, and Wigan Pier is the last of them. The pits closed, the pier fell into disuse and in 1929 it was dismantled and sold for scrap – for £34.

SOUTHPORT (1860)

Southport Pier is the second longest in the UK and, thankfully, has a pier tram. To be fair, the pier tram has a lot of land to travel over before the sea hoves into view. This was a joke even in Victorian times. On an old postcard, two girls are admiring the waves at Blackpool. "So that's where the sea goes when it's not at Southport," says one. In fact, you can see Blackpool from Southport pier. I take the tram out and have a great time in the pier-head amusement arcade. There's a huge collection of old-time penny-in-the-slot machines – Mutoscopes - operated by old pennies that you buy at the hugely inflated rate of ten for a pound. Pre-decimalisation, it was 240 pennies to the pound! But it was worth it. Some of the "What the Butler Saw" type machines are very, very cheeky and would definitely be "top shelf" even in

Southport 2007, pier tram

today's more relaxed climate. Then it's a brisk walk back to shore and on to Blackpool, surely still Britain's premier seaside holiday resort (sorry, Brighton), but first passing through Preston and Lytham St Annes. My walk time: 10min 31sec.

LYTHAM JETTY (2003)

"Lytham pier is no good, chop it up for firewood". My Nana moved – briefly – from Manchester to Lytham, but found it too quiet and soon moved back to Chorlton-cum-Hardy. She and Grandad took me to Lytham a few times, and as a teenager I used to bike there from Bury. But Lytham Pier post WW2 was derelict and was eventually demolished in 1960. Old pictures show a fine pier, built

Lytham 1925

in 1865 at a cost of £5,600. It closed in 1938. Visiting the site, what do I see but a jetty, a small, wooden jetty but still a miniscule descendant of Lytham Pier. A short, simple wooden walkway just inches above the water, it takes you a few feet out into the Ribble estuary, "avoiding deep mud" as the notice says. Apart from the Sailing Club and the RNLI shop, the only other public facility is the car park with its dedicated space for the ice cream van. So Lytham Pier lives on.

St Annes 2007, mock Tudor front

Lytham Jetty 2008

ST ANNES (1885)

Gracie Fields did not make her debut on St Annes Pier, but this was her first seaside appearance, on the sands at it happens. It was 1903, she was only 15 but already the star of the show. In those days showmen would set up a shelter on the sands, put on a show and take round the hat. Somehow I don't think that many of today's stars from "Big Brother" and the "X-factor" would survive in that environment. But then, I'm prejudiced. For me, "live" means in front of a live audience, the one true test of an entertainer. St Annes Pier gives you great views to north and south, but I have to give them a miss this time – the deck is closed for refurbishment. The amusement arcade, the mainstay of so many of our seaside piers, was going full blast. The pier entrance, with its mock-Tudor frontage, looks for all the world like a railway station (but a handsome one at that), while the pier itself retains much of its Victorian charm. And there's the sand, and the sand-dunes. My walk time (part): 1min 17sec. (2008 2min 13sec).

BLACKPOOL SOUTH (1893)

Six Piers Ltd, the company which owns the three Blackpool Piers and three others (so that's where the name comes from!) are busy refurbishing the South Pier. And there's a lot going on at this end of the "Golden Mile" with the promenade being completely rebuilt. It'll be great when it's finished. I contemplated the bungee jumping at the end of the pier – leaping out over the sea, no less – and decided to give it a miss. Adrenalin Zone, they call it. Daft Zone, more like. But it takes all sorts…. My walk time: 3min 15sec.

St Annes c1956 (the sun always shone in the 1950s)

Blackpool South 2007

Blackpool North c1950, sun worshippers

Blackpool Central 2007

Blackpool North 2007

Fleetwood c1947, in its heyday

BLACKPOOL CENTRAL (1868)

Sheltering beneath the old lifeboat house next to Central Pier I find a herd (is that right?) of ten donkeys, "all licenced" as owner Marlen Edge proudly tells me. Expecting him to be from a long line of seaside donkey proprietors, I am surprised to learn this is only his fifth season. Marlen was an aeronautical engineer. He was on his way to Knutsford to buy a car when he spotted a barn and land – ideal for keeping ponies. He and his wife Suzzana ran pony rides at boot fairs and fetes, and moved on to donkeys. Now they have five of Blackpool's 25 donkey-ride "pitches". And 16-year old son Adam is also part of the business, so maybe there will be an Edge dynasty after all. Will there still be seaside donkey rides in a hundred years time? I'd like to think so. As for the pier itself, it too is being refurbished. Like the South Pier (which used to be called the Victoria Pier), the Central Pier (which used to be called the South Pier – are you following this?) is mainly given over to amusements to suit every taste. But the Central still has quite a lot of its Victorian heritage still intact. And it is possible to walk around and enjoy the views. But it's mainly for fun! If you want both, go on the 108ft "Blackpool Eye." To build it, they had to strengthen the pier. My walk time: 3min 33sec.

This is a two-day trip, so Blackpool North is for the morrow. I bed down at the Woodley Hotel. Simple and inexpensive, it suits me down to the ground. Next morning is fine, so I take the opportunity of getting more photographs of Blackpool's three piers before meeting the redoubtable Pearl Mina at her office – on Blackpool North Pier. We repair downstairs for a coffee and chat.

Pearl, an attractive and dynamic young woman, is PRO for Six Piers and Pontins. She immediately sees the benefit of all "her" Six Piers being featured in the book I am researching through my travels, "Walking over the Waves". I have to remember to tell my wife Frances all about Pearl. If I forget to mention this young lady I'd met, and then she appears on the scene at a later date and greets me warmly (as she is apt to do), I could be in trouble!

BLACKPOOL NORTH (1863)

Blackpool North Pier is very special to me. It was the first pier I ever went on. I was six and it was great! Walking over the water, seeing the waves below you through the planks of the pier deck, and yet perfectly safe. But when I asked my Nana if we could go on the next pier I could see (Central), she said no, "it's not the sort of place we wanted to go to". Likewise, South Pier. In my researches years later, I find that the North Pier was always considered "superior" to the other two. So it always means a lot to me to go on the North Pier. Did you know this was where Harry Corbett found "Sooty", the black-and-gold toy bear that is perhaps the most famous glove puppet in the world? There's a plaque near the entrance that tells you so. And by a happy coincidence, I see that "Sooty" is to appear here later in the year. There's a pier tram, taking you to the theatre and the traditional "hobby horse" carousel. If you look at the old postcards, you'll see rows and rows of deckchairs on the pier deck. Sun-bathing is still well catered for on the North Pier, with plenty of glazed shelters so you can enjoy the sun and avoid the breeze if that's what you want. My walk time: 4min 07sec.

FLEETWOOD VICTORIA (1910)

Round the corner, as it were, is Fleetwood Pier. Fleetwood Pier is closed and has been for the past two years. Even the shoreside pavilion is closed. It seems the only way to save the pier, what's left of it anyway, is to build flats at the shore end. That's down to the owner. He just happens to be "adult" comedian Joey Blower, who just happens to work at Blackpool North Pier. I talk to Joey on the phone. "It won't pay," is his straight-forward assessment of the pier as it stands, "that's been proven". Why St Annes Pier to the south of Blackpool is flourishing, while Fleetwood Pier to the north is not, is something I can't answer. *[2009 Note: in 2008 Fleetwood Pier was devastated by fire and all its buildings were demolished. And no, it wasn't insured].*

Fleetwood 2007, front before the fire

Fleetwood 2008, after the fire

Chapter Four

North Wales, Isle of Man

For my next trip, another two-day job, I hit on the wheeze of combining North Wales with the Isle of Man. After all, they are in the same general part of the world, separated only by the Irish Sea. I plan my itinerary. I'll do the IoM first, there and back in a day. There's only one pier on the island, and although it's closed there are high hopes of it being restored, so to the IoM I must go. I've always wanted to go to the Isle of Man, every since as a youngster I used to listen to the TT races on the radio. I had a great big map of the island on my bedroom wall. But somehow I'd never got round to going, until now. Recently I wrote a book called "When I'm Sixty-Four – 1001 things to do at 60+". Chapter One is entitled "Do it Now" so I thought, I'd better take my own advice.

RAMSEY QUEENS IoM (1886)

Problem was, the Sea Cat from Heysham to Douglas sets off at 2.15am, an ungodly hour, but at least it gives me a full day on the Island. This is in the early hours of Wednesday morning. So, crafty me, knowing I wouldn't get back to good old Lancashire until late Wednesday night, I call in at the Woodley on the Tuesday evening, and book in for the following night. With the hotel and room keys in my pocket, I won't disturb anyone when I arrive back after midnight some 27 hours later. I set off with a light heart.

Ramsey Queens c1950, crowds and cars
(courtesy of Fred Hodgson, Friends of Queens Pier)

Ramsey Queens 2007, gates firmly closed

After dining well at a local pub, I settle down at the ferry terminal and catch some sleep before boarding. Again making myself comfortable, I get some more shuteye before we land at Douglas at 5.45am. I catch the first bus to Ramsey – now that's a hair-raising ride – and got to my destination bright and early. But where is the pier? I walk down the nearest street that leads to the shore – you're never far from the sea on the Island – but there's no sign of any pier. Eventually I find a native, but he's not quite sure what I'm after. "There's the pier", he says, pointing to where a couple of ships are tied up. "But it's the Queen's Pier I'm after," I explain, "it's closed".

My informant is more puzzled than ever. Why should a bloke ask to go to a pier that's closed, I can see him thinking. "It's just past there," he says". No, it wasn't just past there. But when I get to the end of the harbour pier, I can see my objective, quite some way away along the shore. It being a nice day and with plenty of time in hand, I am quite content to enjoy the walk. Sure enough, this very fine pier is closed to the public, but there is still much to admire. Now comes the sad bit. If I had but known, I could have gone on the pier. But it was not to be. You must understand that in making my arrangements, I had received a very stern warning from the Isle of Man Government – and remember that the Tynwald, the IoM parliament, is the oldest in the world – that under no circumstances was I to be allowed on the pier, which is their property. But I had arranged to meet one of the Friends of the Queens Pier. The arrangement was, when I was on the Island, I was to ring him and we would arrange to meet and chat. That was the plan. It didn't work, and I blame myself.

I thought we were to meet in Douglas. He thought we were to meet in Ramsey. And I'm usually so well organised. So, after breakfasting in Ramsey, I take the train back to Douglas. This is also quite an experience, but one I had very much wanted to try. It didn't disappoint. Back in Douglas, I make a few calls and check my emails – as one does – to get routine business out of the way. Then I ring. No answer. I ring again. Still no answer. By the time I did catch him in, it was too late. What had happened was this. Not knowing what time I would be there, he had very kindly arrived at the pier at 9am, intending to meet me there. But by that time, I had already gone. He waited all morning, then went to work – switching off his mobile phone.

"I could have taken you on the pier," he tells me cheerfully when we did finally establish telephonic communication. Apart from not meeting up, he and his Friends do me proud with the photographs and information they supply for my book. It still looks an uphill task to restore their beloved pier, but they deserve to succeed. After all, Ramsey has the only pier on the Island. There used to be one at Douglas, but it was shipped off to Wales. Don't ask me why. Back on the boat, back to Blighty, back to the Woodley and a deep if somewhat shortened sleep before an early breakfast at the hotel (I told you it suited me) and off on my toughest day yet – four proper piers, one not a proper pier, and two places where there used to be piers.

Colwyn Bay 2007

Colwyn Bay 1910, looking very different

COLWYN BAY VICTORIA (1900)

First stop was Colwyn Bay. This is a very fine pier, but sadly in quite a poor condition. Much of the mid-pier pavilion seems to be falling to bits. But the pier is "open every day" according to the notice prominently displayed. But it wasn't open. Not on this day it wasn't, but that was no fault of the pier owner Steve Hunt. Hunt, by the way, always wanted to own a pier. So he sold his house to buy Colwyn Bay's Victoria Pier – only to realize he had nowhere to live. So he lives on the pier. Simple. The owner is not at home, but the helpful young lad in the pierfront shop tells me why the pier is closed. "It's a crime scene," he explains, "we've had a robbery." I could have sneaked onto the pier, but I decide not to impede the polis in their investigations into which of the local

Colwyn Bay 1953, different again

tearaways broke into the pier pavilion to pinch the cash in the slot machines. I've seen boxes of coins taken out of slot machines. They're very, very heavy. But I wanted to meet the man who lives on the pier, as well as take a legitimate stroll along the planks, so I gave it up for another day. But my helpful young man has given me a mission. "There's a new pier at Trefor," he says, "down the coast. It's just been done up." I'm very excited. Surely there isn't a seaside pier that my mentor Tim Mickleburgh, an absolute expert on piers, doesn't know about? This would indeed be a coup if I could discover a new pier. But first I have to survey three more long-established piers, Llandudno, Bangor and Beaumaris.

RHOS-ON-SEA (1896)

On my way to Llandudno, I stop off at Rhos-on-Sea. Now remember I told you that the pier at Douglas, Isle on Man, had been shipped to Wales? Wake up at the back there! Well, this is where it landed in 1896. Unfortunately, it lasted less than sixty years. Now all that remains of the Rhos-on-Sea pier is its round, stone toll booth, looking for all the world like a castle turret, which now houses the "smallest museum in Wales". I duly record it for posterity.

LLANDUDNO (1877)

You can't mention Llandudno Pier without also mentioning the Grand Hotel which sits on the shore as its anchor. In fact, one arm of the pier loops around the hotel. Behind the hotel are the sad remains of what was obviously a fine Victorian pavilion which burned down, an occupational hazard for piers and particularly for

Rhos-on-Sea 2007, Toll House all that remains of Douglas/Rhos Pier

Llandudno 2007

Bangor Garth 1904

Bangor Garth 2007

their pavilions. Once a fire starts, the wind whips up off the sea and as likely as not the pavilion is burned down. Did you know the famous conductor Sir Malcolm Sargent started his career at the pier pavilion? My walk time: 5min 04sec.

BANGOR GARTH (1896)

If you have a delicate constitution, and do not wish to be reminded of bodily functions, then do not read the rest of this paragraph. Reaching the end of Bangor Garth Pier, I have to "go." Just a normal, natural function – everybody does it. But on ascending the throne, I can't help but notice, through the planked floor, the waves rippling along underneath. And it gets me thinking. As you sit in the attitude of Rodin's "The Thinker", contemplating Life, the Universe, and Everything, your gaze cannot but help be drawn to the waves whipped by the wind under the pier. By heck, it doesn't half help nature take its course. Headline in the "Lancet": "Seaside piers aid to digestion etc". But I'm bound to say, with the best will in the world, I cannot completely comply with all the conditions as stated on the impressive-looking notice over the "throne": "Please do not put anything other than toilet paper in Toilets. Thank you". If you don't immediately get my meaning, remember I am a paid-up member of the Pedants' Union.

Now for something a lot more salubrious, you'll be pleased to hear, but also at the end of the pier – the tea room. Or should I say, the very fine, excellent tea room. The fare provided by mine host Victor is first class, and the surroundings are a joy with old photographs and other suitable memorabilia to interest you.

Outside, there are the views all around the Menai Strait, including sight of the Menai Bridge which was to provide me passage to the Island of Anglesey. My walk time: 4min 21sec.

BEAUMARIS (1846)

Over the Menai Bridge – a pleasure in itself to an old civil engineer like me – you go along the north side of the Menai Straight to the little town of Beaumaris with its little pier. This just about qualifies as a "pleasure pier". There is a shelter, there is fishing and there are boat trips. Oh, and the paddling pool behind the RNLI lifeboat station. In the shelter – yes, it is raining - I meet a couple from New Zealand. They are here bird-watching, but a more prosaic reason for them taking to the pier is to get a better reception on a mobile phone. Apparently, Beaumaris is a "big shadow" area for mobiles. My walk time: 1min 36sec.

Beaumaris 2007

TREFOR

Time was moving on. Back in Wales proper, I hurry down the Lleyn Peninsula on the road to Pwllheli. Fourteen miles out from Caernarfon lies the little village of Trefor, and beyond that Trefor Beach. There's a pier there all right, completely renovated, but only for anglers. But it's a lovely little pier nevertheless. It was built to carry stone from the nearby Yr Eifl quarry for transport worldwide. There are seats on the sea wall, picnic tables and even a bike rack, plus toilets at the car park close by. As nice as it is, Trefor pier does not qualify as a "seaside pleasure pier". So it doesn't go on the list.

Trefor 2007, brand new deck

RHYL

On my way back, I pass through Rhyl and pop in to see my Uncle Bernard and Auntie Muriel. I remember staying with three of my aunties and various cousins in a caravan at Rhyl, when Uncle Bernard was doing his national service there. They lived in Manchester but retired to a seaside bungalow in Rhyl quite a few years ago. Rhyl is one of many places that used to have a seaside pier, but no longer.

Rhyl c1930

Chapter Five

Kent to Devon

HERNE BAY (1899)

Now for my longest trip: four days, starting from Herne Bay in Kent and going along the South Coast, all the way to Torquay in Devon. My wife Frances is accompanying me for the first two days, so I am a little more careful in choosing our accommodation. We land at the eastern end of Herne Bay, and, with no pier in sight, we have a good look at the King's Hall which could be mistaken for the shore-end of a pier. But it's not, and around the corner Herne Bay Pier comes into view, or at least what's left of it.

Herne Bay c1970, as it was

Herne Bay 2007, imposing front

Herne Bay 2007, missing the bit in the middle

Broadstairs c1910

Deal 2007, fish wrestling bloke, Italian youngsters on right

The shore-end pavilion is there, and the sea-end of the pier can clearly be seen, way out into the sea. But the bit in the middle, actually most of the pier deck, is completely missing. The pier entrance is imposing, and the pavilion turns out to be a thriving leisure centre catering for roller-hockey and other sports. By good fortune, we are in Herne Bay at just the right time to witness a Lancaster bomber flying over the town and the pier. It's the Battle of Britain Memorial Flight, and a grand sight it was. Not expecting this treat, I was just quick enough to get a snap. My walk time (pavilion only): 1min 18sec.

BROADSTAIRS

Travelling on round the coast of Kent, we have to miss Margate, which used to have a pier, and Broadstairs, which does have a pier but which sadly does not qualify for the list. I say sadly, because we both like Broadstairs a lot. Frances had many family holidays there as a child, we spent our honeymoon there and returned several times for mini-holidays with mother-in-law. I've been fortunate in that Mum Foote, now no longer with us, treated me like a son. She would tell me off at times, but to her food was love and she was always trying to get me to eat more.

DEAL (1957)

We book into the Beachbrow Hotel, which happily overlooks Deal Pier. There we find piermaster Ray Norman in his control room. Ray is also a photographer and he promises to send me copies of some of the photographs he has taken of the pier in various weather conditions. "The only pier in Kent" he says proudly, conveniently overlooking the one – albeit truncated – at Herne Bay. Deal Pier is unusual in that it is (a) modern and (b) made out of concrete. Now in my time as a civil engineer I've worked on concrete structures, and they can be unlovely things. But Deal Pier is something else. Its round, smooth concrete legs have weathered exceptionally well, and the whole thing has a pleasing harmony about it. The pier-end café is to be refurbished and when this is done the pier will look as good as new. The sun is shining, and the arrival of a gaggle of Italian teenagers enlivens the scene. My walk time: 3min 01sec.

HASTINGS (1872)

Hastings Pier is closed, but the shore-end pavilion has recently re-opened and there is a good chance the pier itself will follow suit in a year or two. Lawrence Bell, proprietor of the White Rock Hotel that overlooks the pier, is also a Friend of the Pier. We take refreshment at his establishment – well, that's only fair – and move on past St Leonards which used to have a pier, alas no more.

EASTBOURNE (1870)

Eastbourne Pier, with the silver roof of its main pavilion sparkling in the sun, is certainly one of our best-looking piers. By great good fortune, I take a shot of it which ends up on the front cover of my book "Walking over the Waves" – the publisher's choice, not mine. On the pier, there's a stern notice "No jumping off the pier, thank you". They're polite in Eastbourne! And what's this on the pier? A

Hastings 2007

Eastbourne 2007, sparkling in the sunshine

35

Camera Obscura, a device that was invented perhaps a thousand years ago. My walk time: 2min 59sec. *[2009 note: owners Six Piers Ltd have put Eastbourne Pier up for sale. Will they change their name to Five Piers, or buy another one to take its place?]*

BRIGHTON PALACE (1899)

On to Brighton, with its two piers, so very different. Brighton Palace Pier, now called Brighton Pier, is a vast commercial enterprise with a maintenance budget of over a million pounds a year. Brighton Pier has everything you would expect on a seaside pleasure pier. We are delighted to find pier manager Anne Martin most welcoming and co-operative to our enterprise. She shows us some fascinating records, particularly of the many entertainers who have appeared on the pier over the years. My walk time: 5min 32sec.

BRIGHTON WEST (1866)

All that's left of the West Pier is a tangled mass of twisted metal, destroyed by fire and pounded by the waves. Yet Brighton West Pier will live again, say the Friends of

Brighton Pavilion, how it all began

Brighton Palace 2007, at night

Brighton West 1950, as it was

Brighton West 2007

Worthing 1913, pier wrecked

Worthing 2007

Bognor Regis 1909, bathing machines

Bognor Regis 2007

the Pier. The Friends are quite an enterprise. They own the pier and are determined to get it rebuilt, despite many set-backs over the years. And at the same time, Marks-Barfield, the husband-and-wife team who built the London Eye, are going to build Europe's highest viewing platform at the shore-end of the pier. Like the London Eye, the i360 will be funded entirely by private enterprise. They reckon 600,000 people a year will visit the i360 – they'll need them! We stay at the Madeira Hotel on the Marine Parade, happily overlooking Brighton Pier. Next day Frances returns to work and I carry on along the coast. Next stop, Worthing.

WORTHING (1862)

Another fine pier with a particularly imposing front and a fine-looking theatre. The ban on diving from the pier is very direct: "Diving and jumping from the pier is prohibited. Maximum fine £50". When was that limit decided, I wonder? There are few people around, and I am anxious to be on my way and make the most of the day. My walk time: 2min 52sec.

BOGNOR REGIS (1865)

"Jumpers and divers will be prosecuted" – except those taking part in the annual "Birdman" competition. Doesn't say what the fine is. *[2009 Note: due to the pier being further shortened, the Birdman competition has since been moved to Worthing].* Why do I get the impression that Bognor is favoured by the older generation (which includes me of course)? It's nice, it's quiet, and there's a snooker club in the Conservatory which is the land-side pier pavilion. On to Southsea, where there are two piers. My walk time: 1min 35sec.

SOUTHSEA SOUTH PARADE (1879/1908/1975)

Roadworks and traffic diversions take me past Fratton Park, home of Portsmouth FC. I arrive at the eastern end of the resort, and skirt the boating lake to get to South Parade Pier. This pier has been twice rebuilt after major fires, hence its three birth years. Old photographs show South Parade Pier, pre-1975, had an unusual octagonal-shaped sea end. Now it is more conventional but still with its distinctive pavilion. My walk time: 1min 45sec.

SOUTHSEA CLARENCE (1861)

Clarence Pier is at the western end of the promenade, right next to the hovercraft station. This is a sideways pier, built along the shore rather than out to sea. It features a huge funfair and various other amusements, indoor and out. So I take my walk as being the short distance from the outer edge to the promenade. Now on to Southampton where I will stay the night. My walk time: 25sec.

Southsea South Parade 1955, from the air

Southsea South Parade 2007

Southsea Clarence 2007

Southsea Clarence 1900

SOUTHAMPTON ROYAL (1833)

The tragedy of Southampton Pier is that its main structure with its distinctive v-shaped head is still in place, as is its extremely handsome shoreside pavilion. But the pavilion is now to be a restaurant, and the pier itself has been turned into a parking and storage area for the Red Funnel company and it not open to the public. Risking discovery and ejection, I venture onto this once popular pier and think of the days when it was thronged with holidaymakers and trippers, although one gets the impression that these were of the more affluent sort. I bed down at the Star Hotel in Southampton High Street. The tricky thing is to make sure you book a parking space at the back of this old coaching inn. Next day I'm on the road again, to Boscombe and Bournemouth, the twin towns who have a pier each. Now that's fair, isn't it?

Southampton Royal 2007, in a sorry state

Southampton Royal c1930, in its pomp

Southampton Royal 2007, pavilion still magnificent

Boscombe 2007, rebuilding

BOSCOMBE (1889)

I'm first to take a space in the municipal car park at the top of the bank, and what do I see? A building site, that's what. But this is very good news indeed. The local council is re-building the whole thing. Not only that, I read that there are plans to develop Boscome Spa Village with apartments and "super chalets", and – best of all – there's going to be an artificial reef, the biggest in Europe and only the fourth in the world, to attract surfers. And where better to watch the surfing that from Boscombe's newly-refurbished pier? I can't wait. No, I really mean that. I have to get on. *[2009 note: I have since been on the refurbished pier and it is wonderful!]*

Bournemouth 1949

Bournemouth 2007

BOURNEMOUTH (1880)

The council has already done its work on Bournemouth Pier which looks a treat after its major refurbishment. There are "scenic cruises" from the pier – how could they be anything else but scenic? There's the Needles, the Isle of Purbeck, Hengisbury Head and so forth. My walk time: 2min 55sec.

SWANAGE (1896)

This is another pier which is best viewed from the clifftop, with a convenient car park in this instance. Swanage Pier is also a bendy pier. No, it doesn't bend as you walk on it, it has a bend in the middle, which to my mind makes it all the more interesting. There is a small entrance fee, but this is well worth it and helps the Trust

Swanage 2007, scenic coast

who own the pier to maintain it, particularly from attack by the dreaded Gribble Worm. There's lots going on on the pier: people are strolling, fishing, diving (but from the pier, not off the pier – "no pier jumping allowed" - and there are boat trips. I talk to several of the volunteers who run the tollhouse, the shop and the café, as well as the pier itself. My walk time: 3min 15sec.

WEYMOUTH PIER BANDSTAND

The funny thing about Weymouth Pier Bandstand is that there's hardly any pier and the bandstand that gave it its name has long since gone, but it still retains its status as a recognised seaside pleasure pier. That's because it still sticks out over the sea (well, just for a few feet) and it certainly provides pleasure. What is more, it lays claim to being the UK's shortest seaside pier. Certainly it's provided me with my shortest pier walk. My walk time: 9 sec. Now, there are two piers at Weymouth, the other (and much larger) pier rejoicing in the name of the Commercial/Pleasure Pier. "You can't miss it, it's just behind the pavilion over there". But I do miss it. How can you miss a seaside pier? But I did. And here's how.

WEYMOUTH COMMERCIAL-PLEASURE

Certainly there's no mistaking the Pier Pavilion, a huge, ugly concrete monstrosity that I am pleased to report is to have a much-need makeover not to say facelift. But where is the pier? I duly park in the car park behind the pavilion, and look for the pier. It is nowhere to be seen. So I approach a chap in uniform – a car park attendant – and ask him. "Where's the pier?" I innocently enquire.

*Weymouth Pier Bandstand 1950,
before most of it was dynamited*

*Weymouth Commercial/Pleasure 2007,
Pavilion "oh, you are ugly"*

*Weymouth Pier Bandstand 2007,
"washes its feet" twice daily*

*Weymouth 2007, King George III's
bathing machine*

He looks at me as if I was some kind of idiot, or a visitor from another planet. "Why, there it is," he says scornfully, pointing at the back of the car park. All I can see is a row of anonymous industrial-type buildings more or less linking the pavilion with the ferry terminal, but he seems to know what he was on about, so off I trot like a good little boy.

Going through a gap between two sheds, I drop down in to what had clearly once been a railway siding and up over the other side where I find the travel office. On the other side of that a couple of boats are moored. Yes, this is definitely a pier in the sense of a harbour berth, but no sign of any pleasure. I walk along the groin seawards, as far as the security gate. I let myself in, looking for chaps with tommy-guns, and find a very pleasant-looking young woman. For all that, she wears her security officer uniform in a confidant manner. "Is this the pier?" I ask, somewhat tremulously. "Yes, this is the pier," she replies, "but this way is closed". She points to the "tall ship" moored near the harbour entrance. "You can walk round the other way, if you want". To be fair, it is raining and I am clearly not looking at a pleasure pier. I will have to consult with my friend Tim. So I decide that discretion is the better part of valour, live to fight another day, etc. I make my excuses and leave (as the old "News of the World" reporters used to say). I still have three more piers on my itinerary for the day.

TEIGNMOUTH GRAND (1867)

There's nothing fancy about Teignmouth pier. It's well kept and retains much of its Victorian charm. I like the pier's sea-horse motif and the series of helpful information boards. I particularly approve of the sign "do not feed the seagulls." Quite right too, flying rats! My walk time: 1min 51sec.

PAIGNTON (1879)

Instead of being situated in the middle of a beach packed with other amusements, Paignton Pier stands very much on its own and is approached across a green sward which makes a pleasant change. With Paignton the western-most point of this particular trip, I point the car eastwards to get back into Torquay while it's still light. My walk time: 2min 20sec.

Teignmouth Grand c1935

Teignmouth Grand 2007

TORQUAY PRINCESS (1890)

All you can do on this pier is to walk along it, although I did spot a courting couple occupying one of the seats (and why not, pray? we were all young once.) The pier does have its own legs, as it were, but it's built on top of the harbour wall. A helpful young woman at the harbour office explains: "we own the solid part underneath, what's built on top belongs to the Council". Let's hope they don't give the Council notice to quit! So as you walk out on the pier, you can enjoy the sea views on one side and the harbour views on the other. No extra charge, but it's free anyway. The Princess Theatre at the shore end looks to have interesting and indeed challenging productions. The car park and shops are just a few yards away and I repair to the nearest restaurant for a much-needed repast before starting my long journey home. My walk time: 2min 19sec.

Paignton 2007

Torquay Princess 2007, sits on harbour wall

Torquay Princess 1935

Penarth 2007, gorgeous Art Deco Pavilion

Chapter Six

South Wales & the West

Pier trip delayed by flooding? How can this be? But it did happen – after a fashion. The idea was (another of my cunning plans) for me and Frances to stay in Cardiff for two nights, using that as a base to visit the piers in South and mid-Wales and North Devon. I would motor down from Bishop, while Frances would take the train from her London workplace. That was the plan, but it didn't quite work out like that. For a start I was lucky, very, very lucky. This was the time of the July floods, and I travel down the M4 motorway only an hour or two before it is closed due to flooding. Some motorists were stranded for 24 hours or more, and I could easily have been one of them. But the floods affect my dear wife Frances as well. Not only does she struggle to get across London from Westminster to Paddington – which takes her an hour and a half – when she does get to Paddington she finds there are no trains whatsoever to Cardiff. Being a very enterprising lady, she seeks every means possible of getting to me that night (now isn't that sweet of her?) but eventually has to give up.

By then it was too late, and too difficult, for Frances to get back to her "gaff" in South London, so there is nothing for it but for her to stay the night in an hotel in the Paddington area and hope for the best on the morrow. So there we were, supposedly spending the weekend together, the two of us sleeping in separate

Burnham 2007

hotels 150 miles apart. Next day the train link is restored, and Frances arrives at Cardiff station later in the day. Meantime, business is business, and I have to be up and doing.

BURNHAM-ON-SEA (1911)

I decide to start at Burnham and work my way back. Burnham is yet another pier that lays claim to be the shortest in the country. This pier is run by the redoubtable Louise Parkin, who pours scorn on the claims of Weymouth Pier Bandstand to be shorter. "They blew it up, and that doesn't count," she says. Closetted with Miss Parkin, a recent Mayor of Burnham, it is difficult to deny her. This is another family-run pier which survives without public subsidy. "Do you know how much it costs to maintain this pier?" she

Clevedon 2007, brightens a gloomy day

Clevedon 2007, on deck

demands. I don't know the answer, and she does not venture to tell me. Burnham Pier consists entirely of its pavilion, but it is a fine building and very distinctive, Although built early in the twentieth century, its design was inspired by the great Victorian engineer Isambard Kingdom Brunel and reflects two of his railway stations, Bristol Temple Meads and Bath Spa. My walk time: 22sec.

CLEVEDON (1869)

Next along the coast is Clevedon Pier, probably the most elegant pier in the UK. The entrance is flanked by something that looks remarkably like a medieval castle keep, but obviously isn't, and another distinctive building that turns out to be the once fashionable Royal Pier Hotel now being converted into flats, or should I say, apartments. Beyond these stretches the pier deck over its series of arches, which look altogether far too frail to resist the pounding of the Bristol Channel. The sea has twice taken its toll on the pier, which also suffered a collapse due to a test loading on one of the spans.

More facts about Clevedon Pier: it has the second-highest tidal range in the world - 47ft (14m); it has no amusements on it whatsoever; it is run by a charitable trust; and it has been completely restored after being closed. These facts I learn at the excellent museum – which also doubles as an art gallery and shop – in the toll house. They tell me the number of sponsor plaques sold to help the upkeep of the pier has reached 9,500, and that there will be a raffle for No. 10,000. I also have some good crack with the gent in charge of the heritage centre down the road. You can spend a lot of time in these places, so I have to cut it short, but not before learning about the "Barlow Rails" which were used to construct the pier arches.

It was Brunel again. Remember one of his (many) great works was the Great Western Railway. Brunel built the GWR on a broad gauge track. By this means he could set his carriages lower and so make it a smoother ride. Brunel used to work while travelling by train, which in those days must have been quite tough. In the end, Brunel lost the battle and the GWR was reduced to standard gauge. Barlow Rails from the GWR were riveted back-to back to make a strong, light structure. At the pier head I find a hardy couple sheltering from the rain. They've come on a day out from Bristol to walk the pier just for the sheer joy of it. On a better day, they would also have enjoyed the panoramic views. The small but perfectly-formed pavilion with its viewing platform and ornate decoration has a motto: "Vigilare et Orare". According to my schoolboy Latin, that means "Observe and Speak" – in other words, before you open your gob, take a good look at what you're talking about. My walk time: 2min 15sec.

WESTON-SUPER-MARE GRAND (1904)

I had hoped to have an interview with the manager of the Grand Pier, but he had a prior engagement – lunch with Her Majesty the Queen. Now it would have been great if fish and chips had been on the menu, but somehow I doubt it. The presence of Her Maj in WSM did incommode me a little – the streets around the pier were closed off, but that's a small price to pay for the presence of

Weston-super-Mare Grand 2007, pavilion on left before it was completely destroyed by fire in 2008

the monarch. The Grand is a fine, confident-looking pier. The magnificent pavilion at the pier head has all the appearance of a mini-Crystal Palace. As well as the amusements, there's plenty to see with or without the aid of a telescope, Steep Holm and Flat Holm islands, for instance. My walk time: 4min 05sec. *[2009 Note: in 2008 the Pavilion was completely destroyed by fire, but the pier was back in business the next day and plans put in hand to build a new, modern pavilion].*

WESTON-SUPER-MARE SEAQUARIUM (1995)

The Seaquarium, spotted by my colleague Tim Mickleburgh, doesn't qualify as a seaside pleasure pier, but it almost does. It's set on an open structure, over the sea (well, when the tide's in at least), it's at the seaside and it provides pleasure for visitors. It even has a telescope.

WESTON-SUPER-MARE BIRNBECK (1867)

The Birnbeck, the only UK pier to an island, is sadly decayed but still a huge, brooding beast. It's no surprise there are ghost stories about this once-thriving pier of pleasure and excitement. I have a date with the one guy who can let me onto to pier, Mike Davies. Before we meet, I take a shuftie. The turnstiles are still there, but they are chained up and the whole thing is barred and bolted. You don't need any notices to tell you it's dangerous – the pier deck has loads of missing planks. Mike turns up dead on time and regales me with tales of the pier: the two boys who drowned, the water shute, the bioscope,

Weston-super-Mare Grand 1909

Weston-super-Mare Birnbeck 2007, brooding giant

Weston-super-Mare Seaquarium 2007, surely a seaside pier

Weston-super-Mare Birnbeck 1915, with all its amusement

the flying machine, when the pier had its own currency, the gas pipe running across the back of the seats along the deck, the pier-master's house with the bell that rang when a steamer was arriving, how his Dad flew over in a De Haviland Rapide.

There is safe passage along the pier deck, just a couple of feet wide in new planking, for the lifeboat crew to gain access to their station. Mike takes me round Birnbeck Island, which the Victorians developed as the local equivalent of Blackpool Pleasure Beach. The opening of the rival Grand Pier in 1904, situated much closer to the town centre, signalled the eventual demise of Birnbeck Pier. Now the buildings the Victorians put up are crumbling – "another bit gone" says Mike as we walk round – and even the concrete pillars supporting the huge promenade platform around the island are starting to fail. The Friends have a handy office and exhibition area in a converted tram office overlooking the pier. They soldier on, but it's going to be a huge job to rescue this pier, as wonderful as it once was. My walk time (from island to shore): 2min 56sec.

PENARTH (1895)

After a peaceful night, sleeping solo in our pre-booked double room at the Penwyn Campanile Hotel just outside Cardiff, I set off for Penarth on my own. This pier is a favourite with me and my wife, but Frances was still trying to find passage from London and I have to press on. By great good fortune, I arrive just in time to see the steamer dock at the pierhead. There's something very special about a boat berthing at a pier. The real glory of Penarth

Penarth 2007

Penarth 1908

Pier is its Art Deco pavilion. I venture inside the small circular entrance hallway or ante-room, but find the main hall occupied by a children's gym club. I note the pavilion is to be restored and so it should be. One of the young mothers tells me the pier was recently used by the BBC as a setting for the drama series "Torchwood", apparently a "Dr Doom" spin-off. Not having seen either programme, I had to take her word for it. Then it's back to Cardiff to be re-united with my better half. We have the rest of the day to get to Aberystwyth and back. Aberystwyth is right in the middle of the West Coast of Wales. We've been there before, but that was when we circumnavigated the principality. Now we are to go cross-country.

ABERYSTWYTH ROYAL (1865)

Aberystwyth does not disappoint. The town is just as we remember it. But was the pier really that short when we last came? Not only is the pier deck very much truncated, it's also closed to the public. The extensive shore pavilion and other facilities are very much in business. I take the liberty of going up into the first floor restaurant to take some shots of the deck, apologise for not having a three-course meal and shoot off before the attentive staff can object. In the bar downstairs, the man in charge allows me onto the forbidden deck. It's sad, it being so short and all, but at least I get to tread the boards, or at least the steel sheets laid over them. Presumably the planking isn't in very good condition. The deck is largely occupied by a large shed where they make ice-cream. At least that's appropriate.

Aberystwyth 2007, shortened version

Aberystwyth c1925

There's a reminder of Wallace Henry Hartley (1878-1912). Who he? you ask. The year he died might give you a clue. Wallace Henry Hartley played his violin for the last time on British shores on Aberystwyth Pier before taking up a his new position as leader of the ship's orchestra on the "Titanic." Yes, he was the guy who inspired his musicians to carry on playing as the ship went down. Heroic stuff. Then it's up onto the Castle heights for more pictures, then the long trek along the promenade to view Aberystwyth's cliff railway. This is one of the very best of its kind, and I'm pleased to hear that the Camera Obscura at the top of the hill has been restored. The engineer in charge of the cliff railway tells me, because the cars run on standard gauge rail tracks, it's classed as a railway, and he has to blow his whistle at the start of

Mumbles 2007

every journey. I suppose he could wave a flag as well, but there wouldn't be any point, would there? We retrace our steps to our Cardiff stopover. Time for just one more pier the following day – Mumbles.

MUMBLES (1898)

The car park at the top of the bank gives you great views of Swansea Bay, as does the pier itself which can be seen to advantage from the cliff top. To the right is Mumbles lighthouse on its own little island. It can be accessed at low tide, but I wouldn't recommend it. The lighthouse is unmanned and it could be a cold and miserable wait for the next low tide. The lighthouse used to be coal-fired. It was electrified in 1969 and converted to solar energy in 1995. The pier is another family-run business. John Bollom now runs the pier, although his dad Stanley is still very much involved. John's son Fred manages the restaurant. My walk time: 1min 21sec. On our way back to Cardiff I find we do have time to visit Penarth pier, where we are entertained by the Mid-Rhondda band. Then it's drop the wife off at Cardiff station as she heads back to her work in London and I drive North back home, but not up the M4. After the recent flooding, I'm not taking any chances.

Chapter Seven

Isle of Wight

HYTHE (1881)

There are four seaside pleasure piers still extant on the Isle of Wight, and to visit all four in little more than twenty-four hours requires some careful planning. We decide to stay at Sandown, but the hire car we need to get round the Island is to be obtained at Ryde. Furthermore, we land at Cowes. It's a bit like the cannibals and the missionaries, who travels where and when and with whom. But I have my master plan ready in every detail. First, with the wife still hard at work in London, I take the train to Southampton. Then I get the ferry, not to Cowes, but to Hythe. This is Hythe Hampshire, not to be confused with Hythe in Kent. But it's not on the IoW I hear you cry. True, but there is a pier at Hythe, one I was unable to include in my itinerary the last time (to be honest, I forgot!). It was a delayed trip to Hythe Pier, but all the better for the wait. As we set off, I get some good pics of the old Southampton Pier from the ferry.

If there's one thing I like more than piers, it's railways, particularly steam railways. And when I clap eyes on Hythe Pier with its very own electric-powered locomotive gliding up and down, I am ecstatic. Now Ryde Pier also has its own railway, consisting of ex-London Underground stock no less, but the

Hythe 2007, record-breaking pier train

Hythe set-up is unique. Hythe's particular combination of pier and railway make it my favourite pier – but only by a tiny margin, mind. Two people on Hythe Pier make my day. One is Margaret Swain, the cheerful and friendly boss of the pier ticket office. The other is the cheerful and friendly, and ever so patient, engine driver Jerry Barton. The engine and carriages are still the same ones that came to Hythe Pier in 1922 after doing service at a WWI mustard gas factory, and it's been operating ever since. And any pier that attempts to set a world record for line-dancing must have a lot going for it. My walk time: 6min 11sec.

Ryde 2008, former London Underground Train on Ryde Pier approaches shore station – "Mind the Gap"

Sandown Culver 2007, CFW relaxes on hotel balcony overlooking the pier

RYDE (1814)

Back in Southampton, I transfer to another ferry for East Cowes. Trust me to organize my trip to the Isle of Wight to coincide with Cowes Week! The ferry is packed, and so is Cowes. I get some good shots of Hythe pier on the way. Studying the bus timetables, I reckon there's enough time for a quick trip to Ryde before returning to East Cowes to meet my beloved after her day's toil at Westminster. Now Ryde Pier – as well as being our oldest remaining seaside pier - is really something, three piers in one, in fact. The middle tram pier is no longer in use. It is, in fact, rusting

away. The original "promenade pier" is now the car access to the ferry terminal, while the third pier is for the aforesaid ex-London Underground trains. The trains don't just go up and down the pier, they carry on along the east coast of the Island as far as Shanklin. My walk time: 7min 04sec.

SANDOWN CULVER (1879)

I take the bus back to East Cowes, and meet Frances off the (much delayed) ferry. We board the bus that takes us to Sandown. It's very dark and very late when we arrive – not that that deters the crowds of holidaymakers from enjoying themselves. We warn our landlady at the Belvedere Hotel on the sea front of our impending late arrival. She is unconcerned. For many of her guests, if not for her, the night was still young. We are pleased to find that our room overlooks the pier, which, lit up at night, looks a treat. For much of my information on Sandown Pier I am indebted to the Baldock family. Dad Colin is the manager of the pier, and he shows me round. Wife Trudy goes back home for a file on the pier which turns out to be a prize-winning school project by their daughter Clarice. The other person who helps my quest is Station Fire Officer Geoff Pidgeon. He was part of the team that fought the 1989 fire that severely damaged the pier. One man I would have liked to have met but can't is pier owner George Peak. In the immediate aftermath of the fire, announced that his pier would be back in business within 24 hours and would be restored to full health, better than ever, in as short a time as possible. The work was duly completed as George showed himself a man of his word. My walk time: 2min 45sec.

Totland Bay 2007, deck closed to public

TOTLAND BAY (1880)

This is a lovely little pier, approached down a narrow track. Most of the pier deck is closed to the public. Pier owner Derek Barran uses the building on the pier head as his studio. I am strongly tempted to defy the ban and beard Mr Barran in his den (if indeed he was there) but, fearing my wife's objections the more, I resist the temptation. But I do incur the "wrath of Frances", a fearsome thing I can tell you. To get some good shots of the pier I climb up the adjacent bank. There is supposed to be a public footpath, but it is absolutely solidly overgrown with nettles, thistles and the like. As a result, I ruin what had been a perfectly good pair of Marks & Spencer trousers. Now I do have some pants that are designed and built to do duty in rough terrain, and are waterproof to boot, but instead I was wearing my standard black trews - in honour of said Frances. I put this argument to her, but in vain. She is unbending. "You silly man, etc etc". I have some good crack with Steve, new proprietor – with his wife Martine – of the shoreside café. This is a modest establishment that offers homely accommodation for diners inside or out – out being on the pier deck behind the café. I needn't tell you what a good spot this is for partaking of refreshment. *[2009 Note: We have since met Derek Barran and traversed his pier].*

Yarmouth 2007, fishing and strolling

Yarmouth 2008, the dreaded Gribble Worm

YARMOUTH (1876)

My mentor and guide to Yarmouth Pier is Ian Dallison, an all-round good egg if ever there was one. We had decided to meet at the ferry terminal office, and both of us arrive in good time. Not knowing what one another looks like, we hang around like two blokes waiting for a blind date before we both say "Are you…?" at the same time. Ian is a mine of information, with tales of the pier: how angry fishermen, denied access to their traditional landing ground by the pier being built, broke down the pier gates; why the pier changed hands from one authority to another; how they fought and won the battle against the dreaded Gribble Worm; and so on. My walk time: 1min 59sec. *[2009 Note: we returned in 2008 to join Alan Titchmarsh as he officially re-opened the refurbished pier].*

Chapter Eight

Last lap

COLWYN BAY VICTORIA (1900)

My final three-day trip has several objectives: make a return visit to Colwyn Bay, go back to Weymouth and find the Pleasure Pier this time, and check out two piers at Falmouth and Gravesend to see if they qualify as pleasure piers. This time Colwyn Bay Pier is open to the public as usual, and the proprietor Steve Hunt is at home. After all, this is his home, albeit of the standard of "poor student accommodation" according to the man himself. There's no doubt as to his dedication to the cause. The pier café has been refurbished and the bar is to be rebuilt. As to the crumbling mid-pier pavilion, it's going to take a minor miracle to put that job right. Like other piers in private ownership, the Victoria does not attract the grants available to piers owned by local councils or charities. Steve is kind enough to let me on the section of the pier not open to the public, at my own risk of course, but this gives me the chance to walk the boards. My walk time: 2min 11sec.

Heading towards the South West, I get a call from an old school chum I haven't seen since we both left school nearly 50 years ago (48 to be exact). This is the guy who taught me to play chess, CJC Hargreaves no less. We had an exchange of emails a couple of years ago, and he has rung to remind me of his invitation

Starcross 2007, lovely setting, main rail line on right

to stay at his place, which just happens to be in Devon, conveniently located close to my route. I ring back. "Thanks for your invitation, Chris," I say, "would tomorrow night be all right?" Speaking on behalf of himself and his wife – brave man that – CJC says it will be fine.

STARCROSS

I didn't expect this little pier near Exeter to qualify as a pleasure pier, and it doesn't. But my stop-off was nevertheless well worthwhile, and not just for the top-class chips at the local fryers. This little pier – which serves only as a ferry landing - is a gem. It's right next to the Starcross rail station with Inter-City trains thundering past on their way to and from Plymouth, and the views across the bay are lovely.

FALMOUTH PRINCE OF WALES (1903)

Eventually I reach my farthest point west – Falmouth. This is September, it's late and pitch dark. My immediate priority is to find a place to stay for the night. For once I have not booked in advance, as I wasn't sure whether or not I would make it in one day, allowing for my detour along the North Wales coast. There are a lot of yachting types about, and I ask advice. My informant

Falmouth Prince of Wales 2007

points to an hotel just across the road. "There's the nearest hotel but it's bound to be full. All the boarding houses are up that road there". So I set off "up that road there" and sure enough, there are lots of small hotels, guest houses and so forth. But it is very late, and dark, and most of them are displaying "no vacancy" signs which means they don't want any callers at this hour, whether or not they are full. I try a few with lights on and without a "no" sign, but to no avail. Every single one of them is full.

I give up, and trek back to the car park. It's now approaching 11pm, and it looks like I'll have to sleep in the car. The nearby hotel is still a blaze of light, so I'm thinking I may as well try it. Bingo! A late, very late cancellation is my salvation and I get to sleep between sheets after all. Next day I set off in search of the Prince of Wales Pier. I find it. Like Falmouth's other piers, its main function is as a ferry terminal, but this pier also has a café, a shelter and seats, and you can stroll along it without having to catch a boat. So as far as I am concerned, it qualifies as a pleasure pier. I'm helped by a friendly old seadog with tales to tell, mainly about the Americans in WW2 who took over the pier. I also get to take pictures of the pier from the back window of Boots – thank you, Heather and Rachel – and from Marks and Spencer's café which overlooks the harbour. Now it's back to Weymouth, and this time I will find that Pleasure Pier!

Weymouth Commercial/Pleasure 2007, where better to take refreshment?

WEYMOUTH COMMERCIAL/PLEASURE (1812/1933)

How I missed the Pleasure Pier first time round, I've no idea. There it is, sticking out into the sea! And there's an entrance sign at the side of the car park, also missed by yours truly on that first visit. The trouble was, I asked for directions as soon as I'd parked and was pointed firmly in one direction – the wrong direction. And I'm a trusting soul. But now we can put the job right. The walk along the promenade to the Pleasure Pier is a pleasure in itself. The views across Weymouth Bay are stunning – no wonder King George III (he of the "Madness of King George" fame) came here for his summer hols 14 years in a row. Reaching the pier, I climb on top of the old toilets to get a good shot from the shore end. The pier pavilion has an upper deck café which is a good place to take both refreshments and photographs. Well worth the wait! My walk time: 53sec. Then I have a date with the harbour master Dave Stabler. On finding his handsome headquarters, I ring the bell. There is no reply. But there are obviously people in there, on the first floor. I can see and hear them! So I telephone, and the man himself opens the window to give me cheery greeting. He lets me in, and we have a good chat.

WARSASH

I find that Warsash near Southampton has a pier, and so it has, but it doesn't qualify. This pier consists only of a wooden walkway on the estuary, landing spot for a tiny passenger ferry, a pink motorboat would you believe. The miniscule waiting room is also painted shocking pink – you can't miss it. There's no timetable. To

Warsash 2007, ferry shelter "you can't miss it!"

Warsash 2007, the little pink ferry

summon the ferry, you ring the bell and stand on the walkway with an expectant look. The little pink ferry (be careful how you say that!) comes soon enough. The big thing about Warsash itself is its D-Day memorial. Warsash was one of the many places from which troops set off for the invasion of Europe, overnight on 5th June 1944 and in the days following. "For our Freedom" it says. Then it's a cross-country dash to get to the North Kent coast before nightfall. I make it just in time.

GRAVESEND TOWN (1834)

This is a short, handsome pier set on circular cast-iron columns much larger than those of most seaside piers. It is mainly covered by its extended pavilion, also contributing to giving this pier its own unique appearance. Renovation work is still in progress, so I am unable to go the full length, but to me the Town Pier certainly fulfils my criteria of being a pleasure pier. Apparently there's been a pier here ever since the Domesday Book of 1086. Richard II gave the watermen of Gravesend the right to ferry passengers to London. I learned that "hythes" are landing-places, and read about the "long ferry", the "cross ferry" and tilt boats. And I can definitely recommend the riverside pubs. My walk time (part) 29sec.

GRAVESEND ROYAL TERRACE (1844)

Not quite a twin, but very much of the same type as the Town Pier, there's this other pier just a couple of hundred yards downstream. Royal Terrace Pier does not qualify as a pleasure pier, simply because it is owned and used by the Port of London Authority and is not open to the public. But it's in very good nick and worth a look. 190ft long, and set on 22 cast-iron columns, it was (of course) a rival to the Town Pier. In 1858 Queen Victoria's eldest daughter Victoria married the Crown Prince of Prussia, and they boarded the Royal Yacht here to go on their honeymoon. Five years later the pier played host to the future Queen Alexandra and the Prince of Wales, later Edward VII. He strikes me as being a piers

Gravesend Town 2007

Gravesend Royal Terrace 2007

Sheerness 2007, in the gathering gloom

man – fun and frivolity on the waves. There are other historical connections here. You can see the remains of one of five blockhouses built by King Henry VIII in 1539/40 along with booms across the River Thames to foil a possible invasion.

SHEERNESS (1876)

In the gathering gloom, my final foray to Sheerness does not produce much of note. Thanks to a long trek along the hard, I get a close look at Sheerness Pier, but not only does it seem to have been exclusively a ferry terminal, it also appears to be closed altogether. I also make a vain attempt to locate the remains of the once-busy Queenborough Pier. Locals assure me they are there, but I can't find anything. Then as I round the headland in the gathering gloom I find myself almost cut off by the rapidly rising tide and have to beat a hasty retreat. I knew that all that marathon running would come in handy one day! With that, I have completed my self-imposed task of visiting every remaining UK seaside pleasure pier. Tired but happy, I make my way back to London for an overnight stay before heading home Up North. It's a good feeling.

Postscript

I enjoyed my 2007 Pier Trip around all our seaside piers so much that I decided to do it all again the following year, and to try and get others to do the same with The Great British PierCrawl 2008. For details, log on to www.piercrawl.info. Every pier has its own unique character, so visit as many as you can!

- Chris Foote Wood

WEBSITES

To get your book published: www.writersinc.biz
PierCrawl: www.piercrawl.info
National Piers Society: www.piers.co.uk
Coast to Coast Cycle Trip: www.chrisridesc2c.info

Chris & Frances on Brighton Pier 2007, the sad remains of Brighton West in the background

The Great British Pier Crawl 2008

Great British PierCrawl begins at Saltburn, 1st April 2008

National Piers Society members "Piercrawl" at Deal

Penarth, sparse crowd on deck

Southsea Clarence, dad and lad meet CFW

Brighton Palace

Book launch on Brighton Palace Pier

Book signing, Teignmouth Grand

Author Talk, Saltburn

TV recording, Hastings

Two film crews record CFW entertaining on Eastbourne Pier

German students turn "Crawl" into "Run" on Hastings Pier

Blackpool Central

CFW hard at work for the benefit of the press, Weston-super-Mare Grand

Great Yarmouth Britannia, CFW having fun

TV captures CFW's "warm-up" on Yarmouth Pier

Seaside fun, Blackpool Central

Ghost train fun with tv presenter, Great Yarmouth Britannia

*CFW interviews Totland Bay Pier owner,
artist Derek Barran*

*CFW with Alan Titchmarsh at the
re-opening of Yarmouth's wooden pier*

*Southsea South Parade, CFW poses with
Penny Pink of Six Piers, Abba style*

PierCrawlers, Clacton

*A keen bunch of Piercrawlers on
Yarmouth Pier*

*With Pearl Mina and tv presenter,
Blackpool Central*

With Tim Mickleburgh, Cleeethorpes

*Carole (left), Chris and Marion
in costume, Brighton*

Chris and Keith compare boaters, Southend